LET'S GET ZAPPING...

SO WHAT SHOULD YOU BE ZAPPING IN THE ANNUAL?

Wherever you see the **interactive icon** you'll be able to unlock a fun experience to enjoy on your device. There are 15 scattered throughout the book to discover.

See if you can find them all.

READY.

Open Zappar on your device and find the Zapcode in the menu.

AIM.

Tap the Zapcode icon in the menu and scan the code on the page to download the content to your device.

ZAP.

Then point your device at the page and watch it come to life.

A FEW HELPFUL TIPS...

To get the best possible experience here are a few hints and tips:

• Connect to wifi if you can and the experiences will download even quicker than on 3G.

• Try and keep the pages as flat as you can for the best effect. Rest the book on a table or on the floor.

• Try and keep the full page in view from your phone after scanning the code. Don't get too close or far away if you can help it.

• Try and keep the pages clean and free from tears, pen and other marks as this may affect the experience.

• It's best to view the pages in good lighting conditions if you can.

If you're still having problems then do contact us at **support@zappar.com** and we'll do our best to help you.

ANGRY BIRDS

Published 2013. Pedigree Books Limited, Beech Hill House, Walnut Gardens, Exeter, Devon, EX4 4DH www.pedigreebooks.com - books@pedigreegroup.co.uk The Pedigree trademark, email and website address, are the sole and exclusive properties of Pedigree Group Limited, used under licence in this publicaion.

ROVIO BOOKS

Pedigree

CONTENTS

❯ Unlock bonus interactive features!

WELCOME

to Piggy Island

Welcome to Piggy Island,
home to a group of rare birds.
These birds dream of living peacefully
and rearing the next generation of
their species. Unfortunately they are
not the only creatures on the island.
A kingdom of egg-obsessed Pigs also
inhabits Piggy Island. The Pigs are
ruled by the greedy and tyrannical
King Pig Smooth Cheeks who is intent
on stealing and eating the Birds three,
precious eggs. With an army of Minion
Pigs on their tail-feathers, no wonder
the Birds are very, very Angry.

FINDING FEATHERS

The Angry Birds have left a trail of floating feathers throughout this Annual. Can you count how many feathers there are and figure out which birds they belong to?

FREE INTERACTIVE PROFILE PAGE
ZAP THIS PAGE TO UNLOCK

RED

A.K.A The Red Bird

ANGRY LEADER! ➡

CHAMPION ⭐⭐⭐ PIG POPPER

Red would do anything to protect the Angry Birds and the eggs and takes his role as leader of The Flock very seriously.

Fans' nicknames: *Boss Red, Wood Breaker*

Red is a fearless warrior who is always first in the slingshot. He does have a caring side and is secretly maternal towards the eggs. He also helps Bomb positively channel his energies and is the only bird who can communicate with Terence.

RED LIKES:
Motivating The Flock

RED LOATHES:
Delegating responsibility

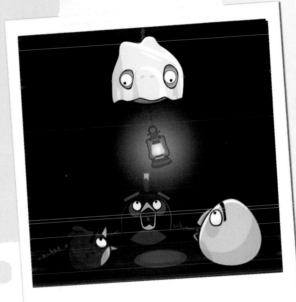

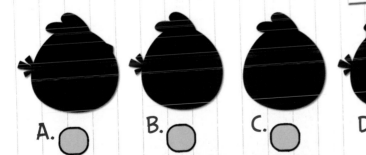

A.   B.   C.   D.

RED RINGER!

IT'S HIGH NOON ON PIGGY ISLAND. CAN YOU WORK OUT WHICH OF THE SHADOWS ABOVE MATCHES THE PROFILE PICTURE OF RED ON THE OPPOSITE PAGE?

CHUCK

A.K.A The Yellow Bird

STREAMLINED FOR SPEED!

Chuck is hugely loyal to his leader, Red and aspires to be like Red; unfortunately he is needy and lacks important leadership qualities like confidence, focus and foresight.

Fans' nicknames: *Lazer Bird, Speedy Bird*

Chuck trains hard at every discipline - especially martial arts, but he's not as strong as he likes to think and without Red's direction is easily distracted and a bit of a liability.

CHAMPION
★★★
SUPER SPEED

CAN YOU DRAW WHAT ELSE CHUCK HAS TAKEN WITH HIM ON HIS PICNIC?

Chuck is the fastest of The Flock and possesses triggerable in-flight acceleration.

CHUCK LIKES: Being centre of attention

CHUCK LOATHES: Thunder and the dark

BOMB

A.K.A The Bomb Bird

KA-BOOM!

SHORT FUSE!

Bomb is hugely powerful and able to explode at will. Worryingly he is not in full control of his destructive potential powers. Bomb has an admirer in Matilda, but finds her attentions annoying.

Fans' nicknames: *Kamikaze Bird, Stone Smasher*

His childish sense of humour makes him popular – particularly with The Blues.
He often amuses himself by startling the Birds with small, unexpected explosions.

CHAMPION
EXPLODER

WARNING!
MAY EXPLODE AT ANY TIME

BOMB LIKES:
Blowing things up!

BOMB LOATHES:
Doing chores around the Birds' camp

HIDE AND SQUAWK

BOMB IS PLAYING HIDE AND SQUAWK WITH JIM, JAKE AND JAY. CAN YOU HELP HIM THROUGH THE MAZE OF BUSHES, TO FIND THE TRICKSY TRIO?

MATILDA

A.K.A The White Bird

EGG DROPPER!

CHAMPION
PEACE KEEPER

Matilda is the 'earth mother' of The Flock. She hopes one day it will be possible for The Flock to live in peace. She is easily offended and cannot take criticism.

Fans' nicknames: *Egg Master, Chicken Bird*

MATILDA'S HERBAL TEA SMOOTHIE

YOU WILL NEED:
- Half a cup of herbal tea (chamomile, green or other)
- A handful of strawberries, raspberries or blueberries
- Drizzle of honey
- 1 large banana
- Handful of raw spinach leaves (optional)
- Ice cubes
- A food processor or hand held blender

When Matilda gets mad she is capable of unleashing a one-bird bombardment on The Pigs, with her enormous, explosive egg bombs.

MATILDA LIKES:
Doing Nest Shui (and herbal tea!)

MATILDA LOATHES:
Anyone who disses her cooking.

DON'T BE A BIRD-BRAIN. ASK A GROWN UP TO HELP YOU WITH THE BLENDER.

HERE'S WHAT TO DO:
1. Blend all the ingredients until the mixture is smooth.
2. Pour into a tall glass.
3. Slurp it while it's cold.

THE BLUES

A.K.A Jim, Jake & Jay

TRIPLE THREAT

CHAMPION TEAM WORK

The Blues are naïve, boisterous and adventurous. They respect and admire Red, think Bomb's explosive tendencies are cool and love hanging out with their hero – Mighty Eagle. Hatched from the same egg, they are so alike they can't even tell each other apart.

There are _____ trios.

THREE'S COMPANY

ALL THE BEST THINGS COME IN THREES, BUT HOW MANY TRIOS CAN YOU SPOT ON THIS PAGE? GIVE YOURSELF 60 SECONDS TO LOOK AT THIS PICTURE, THEN COVER IT UP AND TRY TO REMEMBER THEM ALL. WRITE THE NUMBER OF TRIOS ON THE POLAROID.

Fans' nicknames: Cluster Birds

GUESTS IN THE NEST

The core Flock has some regular birdie visitors. These tribe members are also united in the face of the Piggy threat to the eggs. Get to know their feathery faces well, as you'll definitely be seeing them around!

BUBBLES

A.K.A. Orange Bird

Small. Quiet. Surprising.

This candy-eating cutie can expand like a balloon.

STELLA

A.K.A. Pink Bird

Dramatic. Stubborn. Independent.

Don't let her fluffy pink looks fool you, this is one feisty chick.

TERENCE

A.K.A. Big Brother

Sinister. Stealthy.Massive.
Big Tel is a bird of few
words – none, in fact!

HAL

A.K.A. Green Bird

**Sociable. Friendly.
Free-spirited.**
Easygoing Hal is a
banjo-playing drifter.

MIGHTY EAGLE

A.K.A. Legend

Grumpy. Nostalgic. Guilt-ridden.

Mighty Eagle is a
respected veteran
warrior but is now
a cave-dwelling loner.

PRACTICAL YOLKS

RANK YOUR PRANK OUT OF FIVE!

The boisterous Blues just love playing jokes on the other Birds. Take a leaf out of their tree and set up your friends and family with these playful pranks...

FEELING BLUE?

/5

If your milk comes in a carton, add a few drops of blue or green food colouring before breakfast. Your family will get a shock when they pour milk over their cereal.

EARLY BIRD GETS THE WORM

/5

Before someone you live with hits the fruit bowl, grab a shiny apple, poke a small hole in it using a sharp pencil or skewer, and then poke a gummy worm into the hole. Replace the fruit, worm side down, in the bowl, and then watch your victim shriek as they sink their teeth in!

FOODY FUN

/5

TIC TAC TOOTH

Next time you're in a restaurant and the waiter heads over, slip a few white Tic Tac sweets in your mouth. When he asks how everything is, look pained and say, "It's a little crunchy and tough" then spit the Tic Tacs into your hand as if you've lost a few teeth chewing on your meal! You could also try this at home. Your mum will freak!

RIP IT UP

/5

Drop a coin in the playground, wait for someone to come and pick it up and then, standing behind them, rip a piece of fabric as they bend over. They'll think they've split their trousers!

CRAZY SCHOOL DAYZ

HOMEWORK HI-JINX

/5

Replace your friend's homework with junk paper while they're in the toilet, then gasp as you accidentally spill your drink over their 'work'. They'll go nuts!

WACKY WAKE-UPS

BRING ON THE NOISE!

Turn the volume up high as it can go on every piece of technology your family possess - TVs, stereos, car stereo, radio and computer.

FREAK FACE

Hang a creepy mask from your family member's doorframe when they're asleep. If they get up to go to the bathroom in the dark or stagger out bleary-eyed in the morning, they'll walk straight into it and get a fright!

RUNNING LATE

Get dressed for school on a Saturday morning and shake a younger sibling awake early telling them they're running late! Once they finally arrive downstairs dressed for school break the news that it's the weekend!

HOW ALARMING

Go around the house setting alarms on all the clocks to ring at the same time.

DRIVE THEM MAD

STICKY SITUATION

A member of your family always working instead of taking you out? Creep into their home office and stick the phone receiver to the base, or the mouse to the mouse mat, using double-sided sticky tape!

RING RING

Tape his or her mobile phone to the underside of the office chair, then go into another room and call it. Watch them hunt in vain.

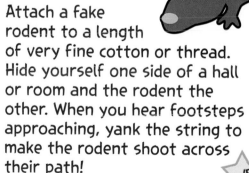

OH RATS!

Attach a fake rodent to a length of very fine cotton or thread. Hide yourself one side of a hall or room and the rodent the other. When you hear footsteps approaching, yank the string to make the rodent shoot across their path!

PARTY ANIMAL

Fill the family car with balloons – pointless but harmless fun!

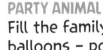

21

WANNA PIECE OF US?

MISTAKEN EGG-DENTITY

It was a beautiful, sunny day on Piggy Island. The sun was shining, the birds were singing and...as usual King Pig was in a massive rage.

So the King's loyal subjects prepared to go on an urgent and vital egg patrol to find the Angry Birds' eggs for their greedy monarch.

Meanwhile, The Angry Birds were blissfully unaware of the Pigs' latest dastardly plan and were considering a day-trip.

Corporal Pig and the Minions had just reached the outskirts of Pig City when a sharp-eyed Minion spotted something.

The troops split into trotter formation and then pounced, certain that success was within their grasp...

The hapless Pigs continued on their way but with eggs on their brains there was more trouble to come...

At last they spied what they'd been looking for. The most gorgeous, enormous egg. King Pig would be overjoyed when they brought back the yolk-filled booty.

They pounced....

Defeated and hen-pecked, the Pigs had no choice but to head back home to face the music from King Pig. Which just goes to show, you can't make an Omelette without any eggs.

THE END

SEEING RED

COLOUR CODE

The Birds are egg-ceptionally angry today because they've woken to find the nest empty. Use the colour code on the opposite page to complete the scene, before Bomb explodes and The Blues boil over.

CHUNKS OF CHUCK

Holy Hawks! Chuck's in a muddle. Can you match the missing chunks of this painting with the place they fit? Find and circle the pieces which are not part of this picture.

BEST NEST

Smart chick Stella thinks
The Birds might fare better if they
could somehow come up with a
sturdier home for their eggs. Use
this page to sketch a new nest
prototype, which would keep those
pesky porkers at bay.

ANGRY BIRDS A - Z

In this isolated cave the Angry Birds have been dreaming about compiling an Angry Birds' Pecktionary. Their thoughts are below, but some entries are still blank. Can you help them complete the list? Pick up a pen and get quacking!

  A IS FOR ANGER.
These Birds are, like, crazy mad!

 B IS FOR BOMBARDMENT.
Regular aerial attacks keep the Pigs on their trotters.

 C IS FOR CA-CAW!
....

 D IS FOR DECEPTION.
King Pig fears his subjects will discover his huge egg stash is empty.

 E IS FOR EGGS.
There are only three, but they're beyond precious.

  F IS FOR FRUIT.
It makes up part of the Birds' diet.

 G IS FOR GRASS.
In the absence of eggs, this forms the majority of the Pigs' meals.

  H IS FOR...
....

 I IS FOR INVENTIVE.
Feisty Stella is brilliant at finding ways to trick or trap the Pigs.

 J IS FOR JOKES.
....

K K IS FOR KING PIG.
....
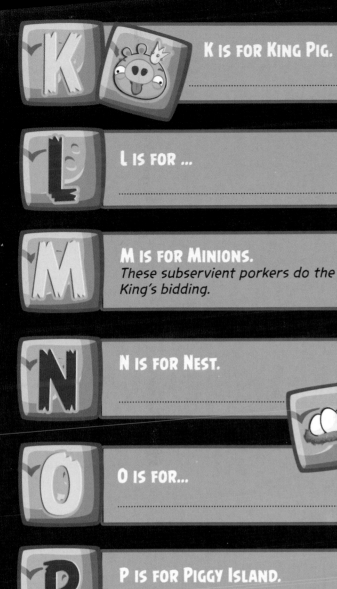

L L IS FOR ...
....

M M IS FOR MINIONS.
These subservient porkers do the King's bidding.

N N IS FOR NEST.
....

O O IS FOR...
....

P P IS FOR PIGGY ISLAND.
....

Q Q IS FOR...
....

R R IS FOR...
....

S S IS FOR SLINGSHOT.
....

T T IS FOR TRIO
Three Birds are better than one where The Blues are concerned.

U U IS FOR...
....

V V IS FOR VICTORY.
Can the Birds achieve this by the egg-napping Pigs.

W W IS FOR WINGS.
Who needs 'em when you've got the ultimate launch pad?

X X IS FOR X-PLOSIVE.
By name and by nature.

Y Y IS FOR...
....

Z Z IS FOR ZOOM .
Is it a Bird, is it a plane....

TWO X TERENCE

You'll have to act quick before he sneaks off!

Terence may be huge, but he's surprisingly stealthy. The colossal creature has squeezed his massive bulk into the grid below. Copy the detail, square by square, into the empty grid below.

PIGLANTIS PATHWAYS

While The Pigs sink like stones, The Angry Birds
are actually quite at home in water. Help Red through the
undersea pathways of Piglantis, to rescue the eggs
while avoiding Octopig's tricky tentacles.

FINISH

37

MOCKING BIRDS

After a long day in the slingshot the Birds love nothing better than to lighten the mood with a joke-telling session. The object of their hilarity? Here's a clue; What's green, portly and rubbish at building things?

What do you call a pig with three eyes?

A PIIIG

Why did the minion pig get in trouble with Foreman pig?

BECAUSE THE OTHER PIGS SQUEALED ON HIM.

What do you call a pig with no clothes on?
STREAKY BACON

HAHAHAHA

HAHAHAHAHA

HAHAHA

HAHAHAHA

HAHAHAHA

What does a pig use to write with?

PEN AND OINK

What do minion pigs do on a Saturday Night?

HAVE A PIG-JAMA PARTY.

What's a pig's favourite card game?

PORKER

What kind of pig knows karate?

A PORK CHOP

What's a pig's least favourite game?

BACKGAMMON

How did the Pig get to the hospital after the Angry Bird's bombardment?

BY HAMBULANCE

Why didn't anyone want to play football with the Pigs?

BECAUSE THEY HOG THE BALL.

What goes "knio, knio"?

A BACKWARD PIG

HAHAHAHAHA
HAHAHA
HAHAHAHA
HAHAHAHA
HAHAHA

MAKE IT
MARSHMALLOW
SLINGSHOT

YOU NEED:

2 toilet-paper inner tubes
2 thin rubber bands
A pen
A pencil
Sticky tape
Scissors

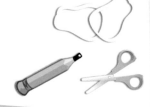

WHAT YOU DO:

1. Cut one toilet paper tube down its length.

2. Roll it into a tube again, so that it's now thinner than before – about half its original diameter. If you rest a marshmallow on the end, it should not now fall inside the tube. Tape this tube together. This is your blaster's plunger.

3. Gently push a pencil through the plunger, about half an inch from one end, so that it makes a T shape.

4. Take the 2nd tube and draw 2 parallel lines straight down from the rim, about 1cm in length and 5mm apart.

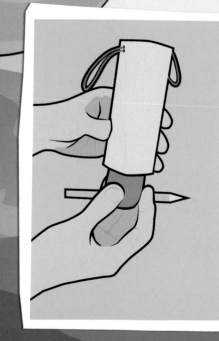

5. Make two slits by cutting each line.

6. Repeat this at the same end of the tube, opposite the first set of slits.

7. Now attach the rubber bands to this outer tube. Push a rubber band into one set of slits so it's hooked on. Tape in place and repeat on the other side.

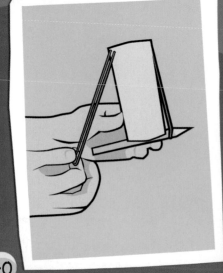

8. Slide the plunger inside the larger tube and hook each rubber band around one end of the pencil.

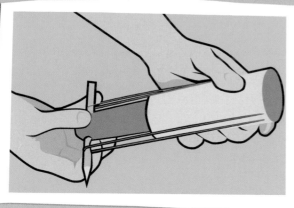

9. Load a marshmallow inside – it will rest on top of the plunger.

10. Hold the outer tube and pull the plunger back to stretch the rubber bands, when the marshmallow is insde the blaster release the plunger.

KA-POW!!!!!

SCISSORS ARE SHARP!
ASK AN ADULT
FOR HELP

ANGRY ANGRY WORDSEARCH

The Birds aren't just angry today...

In fact, there are loads of words for how they're feeling. They are all listed to the right. Can you keep your temper and find them all in the grid?

- ANGRY
- CRAZY
- CROSS
- ENRAGED
- FUMING
- FURIOUS
- INCENSED
- IRRITATED
- LIVID
- MAD
- WRATHFUL

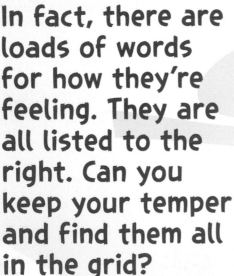

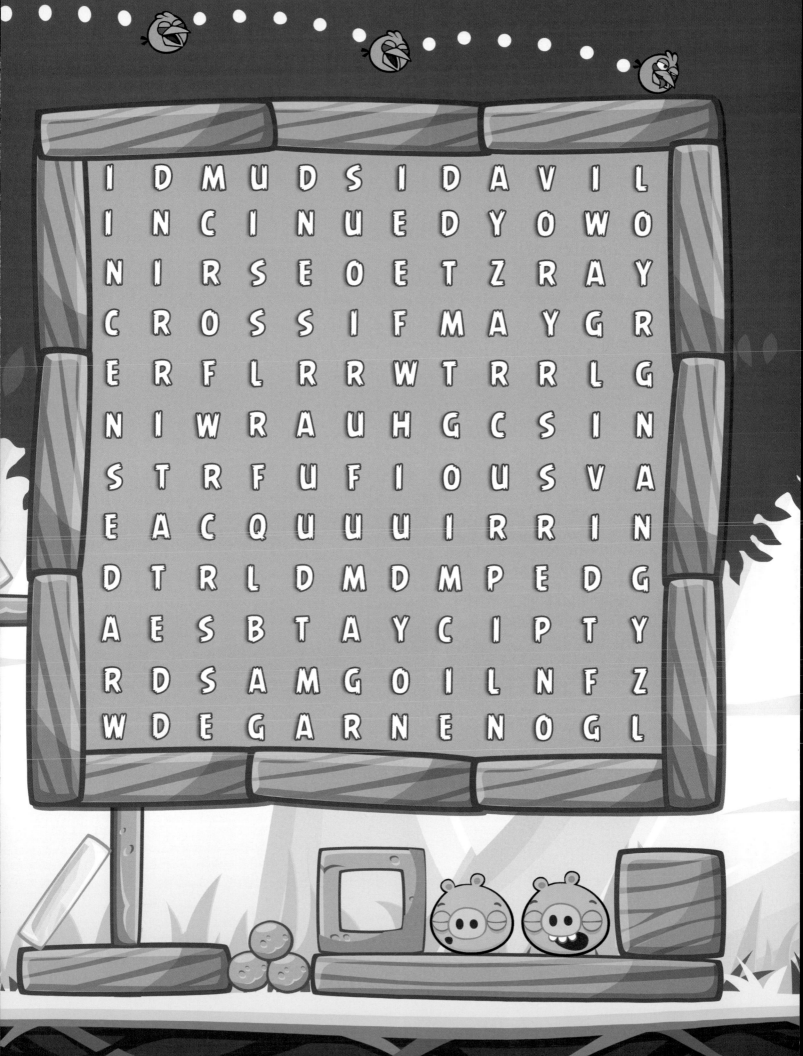

```
I D M U D S I D A V I L
I N C I N U E D Y O W O
N I R S E O E T Z R A Y
C R O S S I F M A Y G R
E R F L R R W T R R L G
N I W R A U H G C S I N
S T R F U F I O U S V A
E A C Q U U U I R R I N
D T R L D M D M P E D G
A E S B T A Y C I P T Y
R D S A M G O I L N F Z
W D E G A R N E N O G L
```

IN SPACE NO-ONE CAN HEAR YOU OINK!

BIRD SPOTTING

In outer space the Angry Birds aren't what they seem...Can you help Ice Bird identify the new superheroes from these clues? Draw a line to match each bird with their statement.

I WILL NOT REST UNTIL I'VE FOUND THE MISSING EGGS.

I AM THE FASTEST IN THE UNIVERSE.

DON'T LET MY CANDY FLOAT AWAY!

I LOVE TO SMASH UNWANTED OBJECTS INTO OUTER SPACE.

WE LOVE TO WORK AS A TEAM.

I'M NOT A PIG!

SWEET SPOT THE DIFFERENCE

Big Bork might look scary, but really he's as happy as a pig in a sugar-coated universe. He just wants to be left in peace so he can munch his way through the sweet treats found in the Utopian atmosphere.

There are 10 differences between picture A and picture B. Can you find them all?

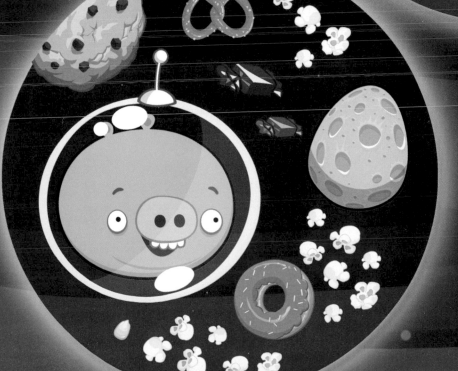

SQUAWK-WENCES

The Angry Birds always line-up for the slingshot. You'll need to use your smarts to solve these complex avian queues.

Write or draw in the missing birds in each sequence.

1.

2.

3.

4.

5.

Odd Egg Out

It's eggs-hausting looking after the eggs! The constant threat from the Pigs means you have to have your wits about you at all times and be on the look out for the merest rustle of a nearby bush. Use your own powers of observation to spot which of the pictures below is different to the others.

KING PIG

A.K.A Smooth Cheeks

GOLDEN CROWN

Greedy King Pig is a fat, selfish tyrant who cares nothing for his subjects and is obsessed with snatching and eating the ultimate delicacy – The Angry Birds' eggs. Born into privilege King Pig Smooth Cheeks is a terrible ruler; mean, needy and prone to bouts of rage.

CHAMPION

PORKY PLOTTER

He lives in fear that the other Pigs will discover his legendary secret egg stash is actually empty.

...and that he has never actually tasted an egg! SHHHHH!

KING PIG LIKES:
Eating Birds' eggs

KING PIG LOATHES:
Being ridiculed

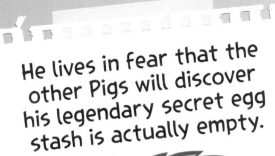

ME ME MEoooooo

FREE INTERACTIVE PROFILE PAGE
ZAP THIS PAGE TO UNLOCK

King Pig likes nothing better than to be flattered. Work out one of the phrases he most enjoys hearing. To crack the code you need to replace each letter with the one which precedes it in the alphabet,

i.e. Change S to read R, change B to read A, change A to read Z and so on.

LJOH QJH TNPPUI DIFFLT JT B HSBDJPVT BOE IBOETPNF SVMFS

....

....

Here's a handy who's who of the King's subjects. These poor porkers are at their mad monarch's oink and call 24/7.

CORPORAL PIG

JOB: Commander of the Pig Army

Loyal. Unquestioning. Militaristic.

The faithful Corporal tirelessly leads his piggy troops from failure to failure.

Stubborn. Self-confident. Incompetent

This bungling Pig supervises the building of all Pig contraptions and structures.

FOREMAN "BOSS" PIG

JOB: Foreman of the Minions

MINION PIGS

JOB: King Pig's devoted subjects

Optimistic.
Cheerful. Clueless.
The lowly Minions
will do anything to
find eggs for
their monarch.

I ♥ KING PIG

CHAMPION
EGG SNATCHER

?!?

The OLYMPIG Games

Pigs love being outside in the elements and when they're not egg hunting for the king, the Minions love to play in the mud. Next time your parents shove you and your pals outside in the garden for some fresh air, why not try some of these fun games?

LEAP PIG

The Minions all bend over at differing heights and Corporal Pig should try to leap over his Minions. Each time The Minions should raise their height until such time as Corporal fails to clear them, then he becomes a Minion and the first Minion in the line takes his turn to leap.

STUCK IN THE MUD

1. Choose someone to be 'It'.
2. Each player grabs hold of one of It's fingers, and 'It' shouts "1,2,3, Is that a Pig I see?" At the sound of the word 'see' the players scatter and 'It' gives chase.
3. If 'It' tags a player, that player is "stuck in the mud" and must not move until released.
4. The only way to be released is for an untagged player to crawl under the stuck player's legs. Players are safe from being tagged by 'It' only while they are in those crawling-under moments.
5. Play until everyone is caught. Then name another player 'It' and begin again.

KING PIG, MAY I?

One person in the group is King Pig and stands at one end of the garden with their back to Minions.
The Minions' aim is to tag King and take his place. They take it in turns to ask King Pig whether they can take a certain number of steps forward – for example, "King Pig, may I take '3' steps forward?" King Pig then says, "Yes, you may." or "No, you may not," and the Minion must do the King's bidding. Minions may vary requests by including options such as taking baby steps, spinning steps, leaps etc. The first Minion to tag the King wins and becomes King.

CAPTURE THE EGG

1. Split your friends into two teams named 'Birds' and 'Pigs' and give each team a cooled hard-boiled egg to guard.

2. Split the garden into two halves – one being home for the 'Pigs' and one for 'Birds'. Members of each team are safe in their 'home' half of the garden, but not while in the other team's half of the garden. Within each half of the garden nominate a fence-post, tree or other object as 'prison'.

3. The object of the game is to run into the other team's territory, capture their egg and make it safely back to your own territory.

4. You can tag 'enemy' players in your territory, sending them to prison in your area.

5. They can be sprung from prison by a member of their own team running into your territory, tagging them and running back, with one freed person allowed per jail break. It is sometimes played that multiple players in jail may hold hands and make a chain back toward their own territory, making it easier for members of their team to tag them.

6. The game finishes when all of the members of one team are in the other team's prison.

55

PIGGY CROSS WORD

Across
1. Pork food-stuff usually fried or grilled.
4. A common sound made by Pigs.
5. Structure built by Pigs to keep Angry Birds away.
7. Colour of skin of Pig inhabitants of Piggy Island.
8. Noise a Pig might make if scared or under bombardment.
9. Area of Piggy Island inhabited by The Pigs.
12. King Pig is obsessed with these.
13. Pig body-part which helps them to sniff and smell things!

Down
2. Fortified house where King Pig lives.
3. Activity Minion Pigs excel at.
6. Curly body-part on rear-end of a Pig.
10. This makes up the majority of a Pig's diet.
11. Pigs love to wallow in this.
13. What The Pigs tend to do in water – rather than swim or float.

WHAT A TROTTER

He's big, he's green and he's really, really mean. King Pig Smooth Cheeks (to use his full title) is a rotten monarch who uses the idea of sharing the eggs in his egg stash, as a way to keep his subjects following his orders. In fact his egg chamber is totally empty – of eggs anyway. Look at this picture for 60 seconds, then cover the picture and see if you can remember the ten things, which are inside the King's fabled egg chamber.

1.	2.	3.	4.	5.
6.	7.	8.	9.	10.

MUD WRESTLING

How many Minions are wallowing in the mud?
Write the number of filthy swine in the box below.

.... Minions are wallowing in the mud bath.

KNIFE & PORK

Chef Pig's knife skills leave a lot to be desired. He's managed to (cough) accidentally slash this portrait of His Royal Porkiness King Pig Smooth Cheeks. Can you save him from royal wrath by putting the picture back together?
Write the correct sequence of letters below.

THE LEGEND OF
FRANKENSWINE

It was Halloween on Piggy Island and the Pigs could barely contain their egg-citement. This, they were certain, would be the night when they would triumph.

Night fell and the Pigs put on their spookiest Halloween costumes in a bid to look as frightening as possible.

They were so busy discussing their pork-fectly formed plan to scare the Birds and snatch the eggs, the Pigs didn't notice a small, pink somebody, eavesdropping.

Boss, Corporal and the Minions lurked in the woods for hours, waiting for the Angry Birds. But as time passed they began to get bored.

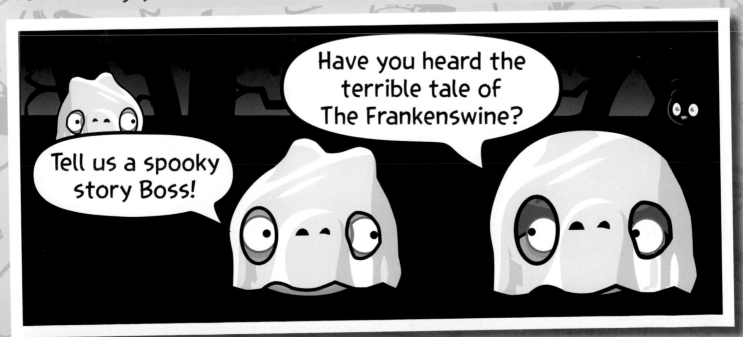

So Foreman Pig told the Minions all about Frankenswine, the legendary pink-skinned monster with an insatiable taste for pork.

Foreman Pig continued his story, recounting how Frankenswine wanders the woods of Piggy Island, stalking his prey.

Then the Foreman told how Frankenswine lurks in the shadows until he spies a group of unsuspecting Pigs.

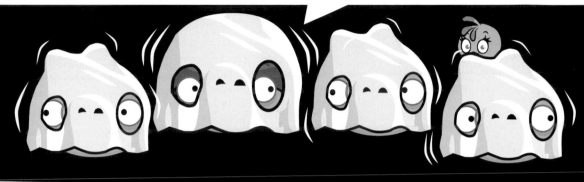

Foreman Pig's story reached it's dreadful, terrifying climax.

THE END

THE PIG-ER PICTURE

The Pigs look oink-fully dreary in black and white.
Bring them into glorious green technicolour,
using your colouring pens or pencils and copy
the colours from the opposite page.

MAKE IT
PIG-TURE FRAME

WHAT YOU DO:

1. Trace the outline of the frame from template A on to green card twice, to give you the front and rear of King Pig's body.

2. Go round the outline in black pen and then cut both shapes out. Cut the centre 'photo' hole out of one of the pieces.

3. Glue around the edges and stick the front and back together, leaving the top and centre open for your photo.

4. Trace the outline of template B onto green card to make King Pig's snout.

5. Trace the outline of template C onto yellow or gold card to make King Pig's crown.

6. Pick out the detail of King Pig's snout, eyebrows, mouth and ears in black pen.

8. Add the stick-on jewels to the King's crown and glue this to the top of his head.

9. Using a piece of sticky tape, add a loop of ribbon to the crown or head so you can hang your frame up.

10. Add your photo to the frame.

YOU NEED:

- 2 x A4 sheets of stiff green card
- 1 x A4 sheet of stiff yellow or gold card
- PVA glue
- Sticky tape
- Ribbon
- Adhesive jewels (optional)
- Pencil
- Black Marker Pen
- Scissors

TEMPLATE A

SCISSORS are SHARP!
Ask an ADULT
FOR HELP

TEMPLATE B   TEMPLATE C

THE WHOLE TROUGH AND NOTHING BUT THE TROUGH!

How much do you know about the world of the Pigs of Piggy Island? Detect whether each of King Pig's statements is true or false – the whole trough or a big fat porky pie!

1. King Pig Smooth Cheeks has a hidden stash of eggs which he keeps to himself.

Porky Pie ◯
Dat's the trough! ◯

4. When eggs are scarce, Pigs eat grass.

Porky Pie ◯
Dat's the trough! ◯

3. Chronicler Pig interprets the laws of the Pigs.

Porky Pie ◯
Dat's the trough! ◯

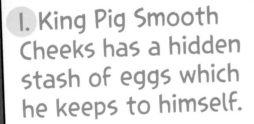

2. Foreman Pig is often known to the Minions as 'Boss'.

Porky Pie ◯
Dat's the trough! ◯

5. King Pig's main advisor is Chef Pig.

Porky Pie ◯
Dat's the trough! ◯

6. When Pigs find gold they attempt to blackmail the Angry Birds with it.

Porky Pie ○
Dat's the trough! ○

9. Foreman Pig is the only Pig with facial hair.

Porky Pie ○
Dat's the trough! ○

10. Pig's love the water and often head to the beach for a swim.

Porky Pie ○
Dat's the trough! ○

7. The Pigs have a wax museum in the Ear Cave of Head Mountain which houses statues of Kings past and ancient relics.

Porky Pie ○
Dat's the trough! ○

11. Pigs are hopeless at building things.

Porky Pie ○
Dat's the trough! ○

12. Corporal Pig is able to lead only four Pigs at a time.

Porky Pie ○
Dat's the trough! ○

8. The Pigs would never dream of eating eggs without permission – they just want to deliver them to the King.

Porky Pie ○
Dat's the trough! ○

HOW DID YOU DO?

Check your answers on Page 77!

1 – 4 correct
A Piggy-ful effort!

5 – 8 correct
Must sty harder!

9 – 12 correct
Squealy impressive!

HAIR OF THE HOG

Foreman Pig was transporting beautifully decorated eggs back to the King, but he got an itch in his magnificent moustache and sadly dropped the lot. Can you work out how many complete eggs he was carrying?

Foreman Pig was carrying .... eggs.

This code runs in the,
Wrong direction.
To crack it check out,
Its _____.

The Pigs often communicate in code, in a bid to flummox the Angry Birds. Solve the riddle below to decipher this latest communiqué.

LOWLY SUBJECTS,
I, YOUR KING AM UNHAPPY WITH YOUR
FAILURE TO FOLLOW MY ORDERS. I AM
NOT A GREEDY PIG. MY ONLY WISH
IS THAT YOU BRING ME THE EGGS
OF THE BIRD-BRAINS, BUT YOU CAN'T
EVEN GET THIS RIGHT. UNLESS I
SEE RESULTS - AND FAST - I WILL
HAVE 2 START PUNISHMENTS ON A
GRAND SCALE. I WILL HAVE 1 MINION
PIG FLUNG FROM THE TOP OF MY
CASTLE FOR EVERY DAY YOU COME BACK
EMPTY-TROTTERED.

☺+○=☆

OINKED
HIS MOST ROYAL PORKINESS,
KING PIG SMOOTH CHEEKS

MAKE IT
EGG-CELLENT
Cupcakes

Chef Pig's egg-shaped cupcakes are, unsurprisingly, a real hit in Pig City. When King Pig is again denied Angry Bird eggs, he has been known to angrily fling the cakes off the ramparts of his castle, at unsuspecting Minions. The Minions don't mind however, as these egg shaped treats are delicious and egg-stremely moreish. They're also easy to make so get cracking!

YOU NEED:

I box vanilla cupcake mix
Yellow paper cupcake cases
Cupcake tin
Lemon curd
I tub ready-made vanilla
buttercream icing

THE OVEN CAN BE
VERY HOT!
ASK AN ADULT
FOR HELP

WHAT YOU DO:

I. Bake your cupcakes according to
the instructions on the box and
leave to cool on a wire rack.

2. When cool place each cupcake
in a pretty yellow paper.

3. Carefully spread the top of
each cake with a generous
layer of buttercream icing.

4. Spoon a round dollop of
lemon curd into the centre
of each cupcake to make
the egg yolk.

5. Place on a plate and serve.

FORTRESS FUN

Feeling squealy bored? Well here's a board game! See what we did there? This game of chance will pit you and your construction skills against your opponent. Who'll be first to finish the fortress?

YOU NEED:

A Pig-loving pal
A dice
A pencil and a rubber each

WHAT YOU DO:

1. Take one page each.
2. Youngest player goes first.
3. Take it in turns to throw the dice and follow the instructions opposite, which correspond with the number you've thrown.

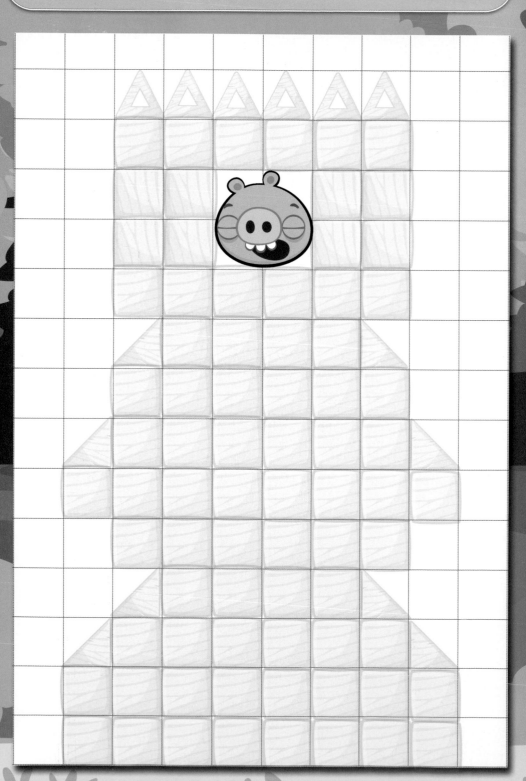

You have thrown the number...

1 = An Angry Bird has damaged your structure and injured you. You must remove a block and miss a turn while you recover.

2 = An Angry Bird has damaged your structure so you must remove a block.

4 = You may complete a block and take another turn.

5 = You may complete two blocks.

6 = You may complete a block and rub out one of your opponent's blocks.

The winner is the player who can complete the construction!

FAREWELL
from Piggy Island

CA-CAW THANKS FOR DROPPING BY!

HOG TO SEE YOU SOON!

FINDING FEATHERS

The Angry Birds left a trail of floating feathers throughout this Annual. How many did you find?

RED   CHUCK   BOMB   BLUES   MATILDA

I found .... feathers in this annual.

ANSWERS

There are **FIVE** trios.

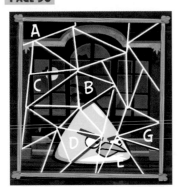

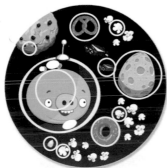

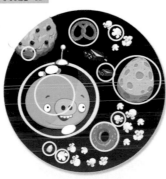

I WILL NOT REST UNTIL I'VE FOUND THE MISSING EGGS.

I'M NOT A PIG!

WE LOVE TO WORK AS A TEAM.

DON'T LET MY CANDY FLOAT AWAY!

I LOVE TO SMASH UNWANTED OBJECTS INTO OUTER SPACE.

I AM THE FASTEST IN THE UNIVERSE.

KING PIG SMOOTH CHEEKS IS A GRACIOUS AND HANDSOME RULER.

Crossword:
BACON, COINK, CASTLE, CONSTRUCTION, FORTRESS, TAIL, GREEN, SQUEAL, PIGCITY, GRASS, MUD, EGGS, SNOUT, SINK

Precious Piggy
Artwork X 2
Vase
Book
Empty Nest
Jewls
Spade
Candy Cane
Hat
Coins

There are **THIRTY-THREE** Minion Pigs

HUNGRY

1. Porky Pie – His egg stash is completely empty.
2. Dat's the trough!
3. Dat's the trough!
4. Porky Pie – They eat grass.
5. Dat's the trough!
6. Porky Pie – They think gold is worthless and discard it while focusing on egg-hunting.
7. Dat's the trough!
8. Dat's the trough!
9. Porky Pie – Chef Pig also has a very thin moustache.
10. Porky Pie – They can't swim, they just sink. They do like mud though.
11. Porky Pie – They can build anything when properly directed. Sadly Foreman Pig is a terrible engineer.
12. Dat's the trough!

Foreman Pig was carrying **THREE** eggs.

REFLECTION

LOVLY SUBJECTZ,
I, YOUR KING AM UNHAPPY WITH YOUR FAILURE TO FOLLOW MY ORDERS. I AM NOT A GREEDY PIG, MY ONLY WISH IS THAT YOU BRING ME THE EGGZ OF THE BURD-BRAINS, BUT YOU CAN'T EVEN GET THIS RIGHT. UNLESS I SEE RESULTZ - AND FAST - I WILL HAVE 2 START PUNISHMENTS ON A GRAND SCALE. I WILL HAVE 1 MINION PIG FLUNG FROM THE TOP OF MY CASTLE FOR EVERY DAY YOU COME BACK EMPTY-TROTTERED.

OINKED
HIS MOST ROYAL PORKINESS,
KING PIG SMOOTH CHEEKS

Angry Birds Annual 2014

Visit **Pedigreebooks.com** to find out more on this year's **Angry Birds Annual,** scan with your mobile device to learn more.

Visit www.pedigreebooks.com

Pedigree Books, Beech Hill House, Walnut Gardens, Exeter EX4 4DH